Non Profit Organization Business Book
Secret Success Plan for Starting, Financing, Fundraising & Management

by

Brian Mahoney

Get Our Video Training Program at:

(Zero Cost Internet Marketing complete 142 video series)

http://goo.gl/gQnSo4

Massive Money for Real Estate Investing

http://www.BrianSMahoney.com

ABOUT THE AUTHOR

Brian Mahoney is the author of over 100 business start-up guides, real estate investing programs and Christian literature. He started his company MahoneyProducts in 1992.

He served in the US Army and worked over a decade for the US Postal Service. An active real estate investor, he has also served as a minister for the Churches of Christ in Virginia and Michigan.

He has degree's in Business Administration and Applied Science & Computer Programming.

His books and video training programs have helped thousands of people all over the world start there own successful business.

http://www.briansmahoney.com/

DEDICATION

**This book is dedicated to my son's
Christian and Matthew.
A blessing from God and the joy of my life.**

Table of Contents

ACKNOWLEDGMENTS

I WOULD LIKE TO ACKNOWLEDGE ALL THE HARD WORK OF THE MEN AND WOMEN OF THE UNITED STATES MILITARY, WHO RISK THEIR LIVES ON A DAILY BASIS, TO MAKE THE WORLD A SAFER PLACE.

Disclaimer

This book was written as a guide to starting a business. As with any other high yielding action, starting a business has a certain degree of risk. This book is not meant to take the place of accounting, legal, financial or other professional advice. If advice is needed in any of these fields, you are advised to seek the services of a professional.

While the author has attempted to make the information in this book as accurate as possible, no guarantee is given as to the accuracy or currency of any individual item. Laws and procedures related to business are constantly changing.

Therefore, in no event shall Brian Mahoney, the author of this book be liable for any special, indirect, or consequential damages or any damages whatsoever in connection with the use of the information herein provided.

Nonprofit Organization

A nonprofit organization (NPO) (also known as a non-business entity) is an organization with the purpose of which is something other than making a profit. A nonprofit organization is often dedicated to furthering a particular social cause or advocating for a particular point of view. In economic terms, a nonprofit organization uses its surplus revenues to further achieve its purpose or mission, rather than distributing its surplus income to the organization's shareholders (or equivalents) as profit or dividends. This is known as the non-distribution constraint. The decision to adopt a nonprofit legal structure is one that will often have taxation implications, particularly where the nonprofit seeks income tax exemption, charitable status and so on.

The terms nonprofit and not-for-profit are not consistently differentiated across jurisdictions. In layman's terms they are usually equivalent in concept, although in various jurisdictions there are accounting and legal differences.

The nonprofit landscape is highly varied, although many people have come to associate NPOs with charitable organizations. Although charities do make up an often high-profile or visible aspect of the sector, there are many other types of nonprofit organization. Overall, they tend to be either member-serving or community-serving.

Member-serving organizations include mutual societies, cooperatives, trade unions, credit unions, industry associations, sports clubs, retired serviceman's clubs and peak bodies – organizations that benefit a particular group of people i.e. the members of the organization. Typically, community-serving organizations are focused on providing services to the community in general, either globally or locally: organizations delivering human services programs or projects, aid and development programs, medical research, education and health services, and so on. It could be argued many nonprofits sit across both camps, at least in terms of the impact they make. For example, the grassroots support group that provides a lifeline to those with a particular condition or disease could be deemed to be serving its members (by directly supporting them) and the broader community (through the provision of a service for fellow citizens).

Many NPOs use the model of a double bottom line in that furthering their cause is more important than making a profit, though both are needed to ensure the organization's sustainability.

Although NPOs are permitted to generate surplus revenues, they must be retained by the organization for its self-preservation, expansion, or plans. NPOs have controlling members or a board of directors. Many have paid staff including management, whereas others employ unpaid volunteers and executives who work with or without compensation (occasionally nominal). In some countries, where there is a token fee, in general it is used to meet legal requirements for establishing a contract between the executive and the organization.

Designation as a nonprofit does not mean that the organization does not intend to make a profit, but rather that the organization has no 'owners' and that the funds realized in the operation of the organization will not be used to benefit any owners. The extent to which an NPO can generate surplus revenues may be constrained or use of surplus revenues may be restricted.

Objectives and goals

Some NPOs may also be a charity or service organization; they may be organized as a profit corporation or as a trust, a cooperative, or they exist informally. A very similar type of organization termed a supporting organization operates like a foundation, but they are more complicated to administer, hold more favorable tax status and are restricted in the public charities they support. Their goal is not to be successful in terms of wealth, but in terms of giving value to the groups of people they administer to.

Functions

NPOs have a wide diversity of structures and purposes. For legal classification, there are, nevertheless, some elements of importance:

* Management provisions

* Accountability and auditing provisions

* Provisory for the amendment of the statutes or articles of incorporation

* Provisions for the dissolution of the entity

* Tax statuses of corporate and private donors

* Tax status of the founders.

Some of the above must be (in most jurisdictions in the USA at least) expressed in the organization's charter of establishment or constitution. Others may be provided by the supervising authority at each particular jurisdiction.

While affiliations will not affect a legal status, they may be taken into consideration by legal proceedings as an indication of purpose.

Most countries have laws that regulate the establishment and management of NPOs and that require compliance with corporate governance regimes. Most larger organizations are required to publish their financial reports detailing their income and expenditure publicly.

In many aspects they are similar to corporate business entities though there are often significant differences. Both not-for-profit and for-profit corporate entities must have board members, steering-committee members, or trustees who owe the organization a fiduciary duty of loyalty and trust. A notable exception to this involves churches, which are often not required to disclose finances to anyone, including church members.

Formation and structure

In the United States, nonprofit organizations are formed by filing bylaws or articles of incorporation or both in the state in which they expect to operate. The act of incorporation creates a legal entity enabling the organization to be treated as a distinct body (corporation) by law and to enter into business dealings, form contracts, and own property as individuals or for-profit corporations can.

Nonprofits can have members, but many do not. The nonprofit may also be a trust or association of members. The organization may be controlled by its members who elect the Board of Directors, Board of Governors or Board of Trustees. A nonprofit may have a delegate structure to allow for the representation of groups or corporations as members. Alternatively, it may be a non-membership organization and the board of directors may elect its own successors.

The two major types of nonprofit organization are membership and board-only. A membership organization elects the board and has regular meetings and the power to amend the bylaws. A board-only organization typically has a self-selected board and a membership whose powers are limited to those delegated to it by the board. A board-only organization's bylaws may even state that the organization does not have any membership, although the organization's literature may refer to its donors or service recipients as 'members'; examples of such organizations are Fairvote and the National Organization for the Reform of Marijuana Laws. The Model Nonprofit Corporation Act imposes many complexities and requirements on membership decision-making. Accordingly, many organizations, such as Wikimedia, have formed board-only structures.

The National Association of Parliamentarians has generated concerns about the implications of this trend for the future of openness, accountability, and understanding of public concerns in nonprofit organizations. Specifically, they note that nonprofit organizations, unlike business corporations, are not subject to market discipline for products and shareholder discipline of their capital; therefore, without membership control of major decisions such as election of the board, there are few inherent safeguards against abuse. A rebuttal to this might be that as nonprofit organizations grow and seek larger donations, the degree of scrutiny increases, including expectations of audited financial statements. A further rebuttal might be that NPOs are constrained, by their choice of legal structure, from financial benefit as far as distribution of profit to members and directors is concerned.

Tax exemption

In many countries, nonprofits may apply for tax exempt status, so that the organization itself may be exempt from income tax and other taxes. In the United States, to be exempt from federal income taxes, the organization must meet the requirements set forth by the Internal Revenue Service.

United States

For a United States analysis of this issue, see 501(c) and Charitable organization (United States).

After a nonprofit organization has been formed at the state level, the organization may seek recognition of tax-exempt status with respect to U.S. federal income tax. That is done typically by applying to the Internal Revenue Service (IRS), although statutory exemptions exist for limited types of nonprofit organization. The IRS, after reviewing the application to ensure the organization meets the conditions to be recognized as a tax exempt organization (such as the purpose, limitations on spending, and internal safeguards for a charity), may issue an authorization letter to the nonprofit granting it tax-exempt status for income-tax payment, filing, and deductibility purposes. The exemption does not apply to other federal taxes such as employment taxes. Additionally, a tax-exempt organization must pay federal tax on income that is unrelated to their exempt purpose. Failure to maintain operations in conformity to the laws may result in the loss of tax-exempt status.

Individual states and localities offer nonprofits exemptions from other taxes such as sales tax or property tax. Federal tax-exempt status does not guarantee exemption from state and local taxes, and vice versa.

These exemptions generally have separate applications, and their requirements may differ from the IRS requirements. Furthermore, even a tax-exempt organization may be required to file annual financial reports (IRS Form 990) at the state and federal levels. A tax-exempt organization's 990 forms are required to be available for public scrutiny. An example of a nonprofit organization in the US is Project Vote Smart.

Governance

The board of directors has ultimate control over the organization, but typically an executive director is hired. In some cases, the board is elected by a membership, but commonly, the board of directors is self-perpetuating. In these 'board-only' organizations, board members nominate new members and vote on their fellow directors' nominations. Part VI, section A, question 7a of the Form 990 asks 'members, stockholders, or other persons who had the power to elect or appoint one or more members of the governing body?'

Accreditation

A nonprofit organization in the United States can receive an accreditation by undergoing a third-party review from the Standards for Excellence Institute to ensure efficient use of resources.

Founder's syndrome

Founder's syndrome is an issue organizations face as they grow. Dynamic founders, who have a strong vision of how to operate the project, try to retain control of the organization, even as new employees or volunteers want to expand the project's scope or change policy.

Resource mismanagement

Resource mismanagement is a particular problem with NPOs because the employees are not accountable to anybody who has a direct stake in the organization. For example, an employee may start a new program without disclosing its complete liabilities. The employee may be rewarded for improving the NPO's reputation, making other employees happy, and attracting new donors. Liabilities promised on the full faith and credit of the organization but not recorded anywhere constitute accounting fraud. But even indirect liabilities negatively affect the financial sustainability of the NPO, and the NPO will have financial problems unless strict controls are instated. Some commenters have argued that the receipt of significant funding from large for-profit corporations can ultimately alter the NPO's functions.

Competition for talent

Competition for employees with the public and private sector is another problem that nonprofit organizations inevitably face, particularly for management positions. There are reports of major talent shortages in the nonprofit sector today regarding newly graduated workers, and NPOs have for too long relegated hiring to a secondary priority, which could be why they find themselves in the position many do. While many established NPOs are well-funded and comparative to their public sector competitors, many more are independent and must be creative with which incentives they use to attract and maintain vibrant personalities. The initial interest for many is the remuneration package, though many who have been questioned after leaving an NPO have reported that it was stressful work environments and implacable work that drove them away.

Public- and private-sector employment has, for the most part, been able to offer more to their employees than most nonprofit agencies throughout history. Either in the form of higher wages, more comprehensive benefit packages, or less tedious work, the public and private sectors have enjoyed an advantage over NPOs in attracting employees.

Traditionally, the NPO has attracted mission-driven individuals who want to assist their chosen cause. Compounding the issue is that some NPOs do not operate in a manner similar to most businesses, or only seasonally. This leads many young and driven employees to forego NPOs in favor of more stable employment. Today, however, nonprofit organizations are adopting methods used by their competitors and finding new means to retain their employees and attract the best of the newly minted workforce.

It has been mentioned that most nonprofits will never be able to match the pay of the private sector and therefore should focus their attention on benefits packages, incentives and implementing pleasurable work environments. A good environment is ranked higher than salary and pressure of work. NPOs are encouraged to pay as much as they are able and offer a low-stress work environment that the employee can associate him or herself positively with. Other incentives that should be implemented are generous vacation allowances or flexible work hours.

In the United States, two of the wealthiest nonprofit organizations are the Bill and Melinda Gates Foundation, which has an endowment of US$38 billion, and the Howard Hughes Medical Institute originally funded by Hughes Aircraft prior to divestiture, which has an endowment of approximately $14.8 billion.

Outside the United States, another large NPO is the British Wellcome Trust, which is a 'charity' by British usage. See: List of wealthiest foundations. Note that this assessment excludes universities, at least a few of which have assets in the tens of billions of dollars. For example; List of U.S. colleges and universities by endowment.

Measuring an NPO by its monetary size has obvious limitations, as the power and significance of NPOs are defined by more qualitative measurements such as effectiveness at performing charitable missions.

Some NPOs that are particularly well known, often for the charitable or social nature of their activities performed over a long period, include Amnesty International, Oxfam, Rotary International, Kiwanis International, Carnegie Corporation of New York, Nourishing USA, DEMIRA Deutsche Minenräumer (German Mine Clearers), FIDH International Federation for Human Rights, Goodwill Industries, United Way, ACORN (now defunct), Habitat for Humanity, Teach For America, the Red Cross and Red Crescent organizations, UNESCO, IEEE, INCOSE, World Wide Fund for Nature, Heifer International, Translators Without Borders and SOS Children's Villages.

However, there are also millions of smaller NPOs that provide social services and relief efforts to people throughout the world. There are more than 1.6 million NPOs in the United States alone, and millions more informal, community-based entities, which Frumkin and others consider part of the nonprofit sector.

There are also examples, for instance in Ireland of NGO umbrella organizations bringing about a degree of self-regulation in the NGO sector.

UNITED STATES NON PROFIT LAWS

United States non-profit laws relate to taxation, the special problems of an organization which does not have profit as its primary motivation, and prevention of charitable fraud. Some non-profit organizations can broadly be described as "charities" — like the American Red Cross. Some are strictly for the private benefit of the members — like country clubs, or condominium associations. Others fall somewhere in between — like labor unions, chambers of commerce, or cooperative electric companies. Each presents unique legal issues.

Taxation

If an organization is to qualify for tax exempt status, the organization's (a) charter — if a not-for-profit corporation — or (b) trust instrument — if a trust — or (c) articles of association — if an association — must specify that no part of its assets shall benefit any of persons who are members, directors, officers or agents (its principals). As well the organization must have a legal, charitable purpose, i.e. the organization must be created to support educational, religious, or charitable activities. These elements do not mean that the organization cannot pay employees or contractors for work or services they render to the organization. This limitation means that as long as the organization operates within its exempt purposes and it maintains an endowment or uses any excess revenue to further develop its activities it will not be taxed by the Internal Revenue Service.

Such a surplus — that is, whatever part of its income is left after its operating expenses are paid — which might be considered similar to "profit" — must be spent on the charitable or public purpose(s) for which it was organized, not paid as a dividend or benefit to anyone associated with running or organizing it.

Federal taxes

Not only must the organization meet the requirements the state where it is organized sets for non-profits, but it must also meet complex IRS regulations. These regulations are used not only to determine if the organization is exempt from tax under the organization's activities as a non-profit organization. If the organization purpose is one of those described in §501(c)(3) of the Internal Revenue Code, it may apply for a ruling that donations to it are tax deductible to the persons or business entities who make them. The organization itself will be exempt from taxation as long as it does not engage in unrelated business activities. Such organizations are then required to file Form 990.

As well the IRS has enacted intermediate sanctions should the members of the organization engage in practices that may excessively benefit any of the organization's members (or officers, directors, etc.) rather than revoking the organization's exempt status (which was the only option available before the adoption of intermediate sanctions) the IRS may now levy a penalty on the organization for engaging in a transaction that resulted in a private inurement or private benefit.

Differing requirements at the state and federal levels

Due to differing requirements by the states and the federal government, it is possible to be recognized as a non-profit organization by the state, but not by the federal government. Such an organization would be exempt from state taxes, but not from federal taxes. This may actually be desirable in certain limited circumstances. For example, federally tax-exempt organizations are generally prohibited from influencing elections and legislation, whereas the state may or may not prohibit non-profits from that activity. If you wish to receive grants and donations, it is generally necessary to be a federally recognized non-profit (i.e. 501(c)(3) or similar designation). Contributions made to federally recognized non-profits (such as 501(c)(3) entities) would typically be tax deductible for the person or entity giving the donation. In other words, if the federal court decides that a non-profit organization is acting contrary to the laws, its taxation benefits may be permanently revoked.

Organization

Non-profit organizations in the United States are, like for-profit corporations, mostly organized and operated under the law of a state, rather than the federal government. There are some federally chartered charities, though, including the American Red Cross, the National FFA Organization, the Boy Scouts of America, and the United States Olympic Committee.

Generally, non-profits and people operating non-profits must comply with all of the same laws which would apply to for-profit businesses. There are exceptions for taxes (noted above) and some exceptions related to First Amendment concerns, noted below. Directors and officers of non-profits owe a fiduciary duty to the non-profit and its beneficiaries similar to the duties owed by directors and officers of for-profit corporations. Non-profits can have vicarious liability for injuries caused by their employees or volunteers to third parties, such as by traffic accidents. For this reason it is prudent for any non-profit to obtain liability insurance. Non-profits which have paid staff must comply with minimum wage laws, and with the requirement in most states to obtain workers compensation insurance.

Churches and religious non-profits are something of a special case, because the First Amendment to the U.S. Constitution forbids the government making a law "respecting an establishment of religion" and also forbids "prohibiting the free exercise thereof [that is, of religion]." The First Amendment originally bound only the U.S. Federal Government, but by incorporation through the 14th Amendment, also binds state and local governments. Under the Religious Freedom Restoration Act many generally applicable state laws regarding employment, zoning and the like are relaxed for churches.

Similarly, some non-profits, as private organizations, are not subject to the anti-discrimination laws which might apply to similar organizations serving the public for profit. As an example, the Boy Scouts of America do not allow girls as Cub Scouts or Boy Scouts, and the courts have held this does not violate anti-discrimination laws.

Charity non-profits face many of the same challenges of corporate governance which face large, publicly traded corporations. Fundamentally, the challenges arise from the "agency problem" - the fact that the management which controls the charity is necessarily different from the people who the charity is designed to benefit.

In a non-profit corporation, the "agency problem" is even more difficult than in the for-profit sector, because the management of a non-profit is not even theoretically subject to removal by the charitable beneficiaries. The board of directors of most charities is self-perpetuating, with new members chosen by vote of the existing members.

Charitable fraud prevention

In the United States, prevention of charitable fraud is mostly a function of state governments, and laws vary widely from state to state. Approximately 45 states have laws regulating charities and require registration before soliciting donations.

Fundraising

Fundraising or fund raising (also known as "development") is the process of gathering voluntary contributions of money or other resources, by requesting donations from individuals, businesses, charitable foundations, or governmental agencies (see also crowd funding). Although fundraising typically refers to efforts to gather money for non-profit organizations, it is sometimes used to refer to the identification and solicitation of investors or other sources of capital for for-profit enterprises.

Traditionally, fundraising consisted mostly of asking for donations on the street or at people's doors, and this is experiencing very strong growth in the form of face-to-face fundraising, but new forms of fundraising, such as online fundraising, have emerged in recent years, though these are often based on older methods such as grassroots fundraising.

Organizations

Fundraising is a significant way that non-profit organizations may obtain the money for their operations. These operations can involve a very broad array of concerns such as religious or philanthropic groups such as research organizations, public broadcasters, political campaigns and environmental issues.

Some examples of charitable organizations include student scholarship merit awards for athletic or academic achievement, humanitarian concerns, disaster relief, human rights, research, and other social issues.

Professional fundraisers

Many non-profit organizations take advantage of the services of professional fundraisers. These fundraisers may be paid for their services either through fees unrelated to the amounts of money to be raised, or by retaining a percentage of raised funds (percentage-based compensation). The latter approach is expressly forbidden under the Code of Ethics of the Association of Fundraising Professionals (AFP), a professional membership body. However, by far the most common practice of American non-profits is to employ a staff person whose main responsibility is fund raising. This person is paid a salary like any other employee, and is usually a part of the top management staff of the organization.

Some non-profit organizations nonetheless engage fundraisers who are paid a percentage of the funds they raise. In the United States, this ratio of funds retained to funds passed on to the non-profit is subject to reporting to a number of state's Attorneys General or Secretaries of state. This ratio is highly variable and subject to change over time and place, and it is a point of contention between a segment of the general public and the non-profit organizations.

The term "professional fundraiser" is in many cases a legislated term referring to third-party firms whose services are contracted for, whereas "fundraising professionals" or development officers are often individuals or staff at charitable non-profits. Although potentially confusing, the distinction is an important one to note.

Fundraising professionals, who have been employed with not-for-profit organizations as fundraisers or as fundraising consultants, for at least sixty (60) months, can become certified as a Certified Fund Raising Executive (CFRE). The CFRE credential is administered by CFRE International, an independent 501(c)6 whose sole mission is dedicated to setting standards in philanthropy through a valid and reliable certification process.

A specialty within the fundraising profession is the "grant professional." Grant professionals with at least three years experience, and other requirements, can become certified as Grant Professional Certified (GPC). The GPC credential is administered by Grant Professionals Certification Institute, whose mission is to strengthen the nonprofit sector's ability to pursue and maintain public sector and private sector funding by promoting competency and ethical practices within the field of grantsmanship. The certification process is designed to measure minimum knowledge and skills related to all aspects of grant development and management, including but not limited to such areas as grant research or pre-production, grant construction, grant reporting, public sector funding, private sector funding, ethics and grant accountability.

Religious organizations

Equally important are fundraising efforts by virtually every recognized religious group throughout the world. These efforts are organized on a local, national, and global level. Sometimes, such funds will go exclusively toward assisting the basic needs of others, while money may at other times be used only for evangelism or proselytism. Usually, religious organizations mix the two, which can sometimes cause tension.

Political campaigns

US President Barack Obama's campaign team organised a record-breaking fundraising effort in 2008 based on grassroots fundraising

Fundraising also plays a major role in political campaigns. This fact, despite numerous campaign finance reform laws, continues to be a highly controversial topic in American politics. Political action committees (PACs) are the best-known organizations that back candidates and political parties, though others such as 527 groups also have an impact. Some advocacy organizations conduct fundraising for-or-against policy issues in an attempt to influence legislation.

Public broadcasting

While public broadcasters are completely government-funded in much of the world, there are many countries where some funds must come from donations from the public. In the United States less than 15% of local public broadcasting stations' funding comes from the federal government. Pledge drives, a type of annual giving, commonly occur about three times each year, usually lasting one to two weeks each time. Viewership and listenership often declines significantly during funding periods, so special programming may be aired in order to keep regular viewers and listeners interested.

Taxation

Organizations in the United States established for charitable purposes are allowed to raise funds from many sources. They are given a specific designation by the Internal Revenue Service (IRS), commonly noted as 501(c)(3) organizations. Other nonprofits such as fraternal associations have different IRS designations, and may or may not be eligible to raise funds. Financial information on many nonprofits, including all nonprofits that file annual IRS 990 forms is available from GuideStar.

Types

Many non-profit organizations receive some annual funding from a financial endowment, which is a sum of money that is invested to generate an annual return. Although endowments may be created when a sizable gift is received from an individual or family, often as directed in a will upon the death of a family member, they more typically are the result of many gifts over time from a variety of sources. When an organization has an endowment, it is good practice to keep the endowment fund at no more than 30% of the annual budget. If the endowment exceeds this amount it presents the issue to donors and funders that the origination is not using its resources to meet its mission effectively and is sitting on usable funds instead of supporting its constituents.

Non-profit organizations also raise funds through competing for grant funding. Grants are offered by governmental units and private foundations/ charitable trusts to non-profit organizations for the benefit of all parties to the transaction.

A capital campaign is when fundraising is conducted to raise major sums for a building or endowment, and generally keep such funds separate from operating funds. These campaigns encourage donors to give more than they would normally give and tap donors, especially corporations and foundations who would not otherwise give. A capital campaign normally begins with a private phase before launching a public appeal.

Charitable giving by corporations is estimated to be $15.29 billion in 2010. This consists of corporate grants as well as matching gift and volunteer grants. 65% of Fortune 500 companies offer employee matching gift programs and 40% offer volunteer grant programs. These are charitable giving programs set up by corporations in which the company matches donations made by employees to eligible nonprofit organizations or provides grants to eligible nonprofit organizations as way to recognize and promote employee volunteerism.

Special events are another method of raising funds. These range from formal dinners to benefit concerts to walkathons. Events are used to increase visibility and support for an organization as well as raising funds. Events can feature activities for the group such as speakers, a dance, an outing or entertainment, to encourage group participation and giving. Events can also include fundraising methods such as a raffle or charity auction. Events often feature notable sponsors or honoree. Events often feature a charity "ad book" as a program guide for the event, but more importantly, as another fundraiser providing members, supporters and vendors to show their support of and to the group at the event by way of placing an ad-like page, 1/2 page, 1/4 page, stating or showing support. Events and their associated fundraisers can be a major source of a groups revenue, visibility and donor relations.

While fundraising often involves the donation of money as an out-right gift, money may also be generated by selling a product of some kind, also known as product fundraising. Girl Scouts of the USA are well known for selling cookies in order to generate funds. It is also common to see on-line impulse sales links to be accompanied by statements that a proportion of proceeds will be directed to a particular charitable foundation.

Tax law may require differentiating between the cost of an item verses its gift value, such as a $100.00 per person dinner, for a $25.00 cost meal. Fundraising often involves recognition to the donor, such as naming rights or adding donors to an honor roll or other general recognition. Charity Ad Books are another form of donation for recognition, sponsorship or selling of ads often in an event related program or group directory.

When goods or professional services are donated to an organization rather than cash, this is called an in-kind gift.

A number of charities and non-profit organizations are increasingly using the internet as a means to raise funds; this practice is referred to as online fundraising. For example, the NSPCC operates a search engine which generates funds via Pay per click links, and Better The World operates tools allowing funds to be raised via members viewing ethical ads on a browser sidebar and/or blog widget. Save the Children's Dave Hartman wrote after the $1 Million Operation Sharecraft online campaign, "We may have reached our mark, but this is just the beginning of a new era of fundraising and using social media and digital technology to better the world."

Some of the most substantial fundraising efforts in the United States are conducted by colleges and universities. Commonly the fundraising, or "development" / "advancement," program, makes a distinction between annual fund appeals and major campaigns. Most institutions use professional development officers to conduct superior fundraising appeals for both the entire institution or individual colleges and departments. Examples of this include athletics and libraries.

The donor base (often called a file) for higher education includes alumni, parents, friends, private foundations, and corporations. Gifts of appreciated property are important components of such efforts because the tax advantage they confer on the donor encourages larger gifts. The process of soliciting appreciated assets is called planned giving.

The classic development program at institutions of higher learning include prospect identification, prospect research and verification of the prospect's viability, cultivation, solicitation, and finally stewardship, the latter being the process of keeping donors informed about how past support has been used.

Accountable fundraising

Some non-profit organizations demonstrate greater accountability by showing donors the direct impact of their fundraising efforts. This accountability usually comes in the form of a vote, where the members select a specific program or charity that they would like their money to go to. A specific example of accountable fundraising is the organization Better The World which allows members to select the charity which receives the money they have raised; members can constantly keep track of the amount raised on the browser sidebar tool.

Fundraiser events

A fundraiser is an event or campaign whose primary purpose is to raise money for a cause, charity or non-profit organization. Fundraisers often benefit charitable, non-profit, religious, or non-governmental organizations, though there are also fundraisers that benefit for-profit companies and individuals.

One specific type of event is the "ad book" fundraiser, where those who wish to give funds to a fundraising group do so through the sponsorship or statement within a book of advertisements.

Online fundraising pages have become very popular for people taking part in activities such as marathon running. Those pages facilitate online payments in support of the charity event.

Popular charity fundraisers in major American cities include lavish black-tie gala benefit dinners that honor celebrities, philanthropists, and business leaders who help to fundraise for the event's goals through solicitations of their social and business connections.

Relationship building

Often called donor cultivation, relationship building is the foundation on which most fundraising takes place. Most development strategies divide donors into categories based on annual gifts. For instance, major donors are those that give at the highest level of the organization's fundraising scale and mid-level donors are in the middle.

More sophisticated strategies use tools to overlay demographic and other market segmentation data against their database of donors in order to more precisely customize communication and more effectively target resources. Research by Peter Maple in the UK shows that charities generally underinvest in good marketing research spending around a quarter of what an equivalent sized for profit company might spend.

Donor relations and stewardship professionals support fundraisers by recognizing and thanking donors, and demonstrating the impact of their donations in a fashion that will cultivate future giving to nonprofit organizations.

Recent research by Adrian Sargeant and the Association of Fundraising Professionals' Fundraising Effectiveness Project suggests the sector has a long way to go in improving the quality of donor relations. The sector generally loses 50–60% of its newly acquired donors between their first and second donations and one in three, year on year thereafter. The economics of regular or sustained giving are rather different, but even then organizations routinely lose 30% of their donors from one year to the next.

Capital campaigns

A capital campaign is "an intensive fundraising effort designed to raise a specified sum of money within a defined time period to meet the varied asset-building needs of an organization". Asset-building activities include the construction, renovation or expansion of facilities (for example, a new building), the acquisition or improvement of land, equipment, or other items, and additions to a financial endowment.

Two characteristics set capital campaigns apart from other forms of fund-raising activities. First, "the gifts solicited are much larger than those generally sought during an annual fund". Second, "pledges are emphasized as commitments payable over a number of years convenient to the donor or through the transfer of appreciated real or personal property".

Various types of capital campaigns have been identified. The traditional "brick and mortar" campaign, focused on building construction or improvements, was considered a "once in a lifetime" campaign in the past because of the ambitious goals of the campaign. Today, however, organizations frequently schedule capital campaigns every five to ten years, and "the megagoals announced by large institutions often are the result of 'counting everything' during a five-to seven-year campaign period".

A second type of capital campaign is the comprehensive, integrated, or total development campaign, which aims for a longer fund-raising program based on a long-term analysis of the organization's needs and direction. This form of capital campaign includes ordinary fund-raising actives, such as annual gift drives, which are "slower-paced and lack the intensity of the traditional capital campaign".

Other information

Many NPOs often use the .org or .us (or the CCTLD of their respective country) or .edu top-level domain (TLD) when selecting a domain name to differentiate themselves from more commercial entities, which typically use the .com space.

In the traditional domain noted in RFC 1591, .org is for 'organizations that didn't fit anywhere else' in the naming system, which implies that it is the proper category for non-commercial organizations if they are not governmental, educational, or one of the other types with a specific TLD. It is not designated specifically for charitable organizations or any specific organizational or tax-law status, however; it encompasses anything that is not classifiable as another category. Currently, no restrictions are enforced on registration of .com or .org, so one can find organizations of all sorts in either of these domains, as well as other top-level domains including newer, more specific ones which may apply to particular sorts of organization including .museum for museums and .coop for cooperatives. Organizations might also register by the appropriate country code top-level domain for their country.

Conclusion

Instead of being defined by 'non' words, some organizations are suggesting new, positive-sounding terminology to describe the sector. The term 'civil society organization' (CSO) has been used by a growing number of organizations, including the Center for the Study of Global Governance. The term 'citizen sector organization' (CSO) has also been advocated to describe the sector – as one of citizens, for citizens – by organizations including Ashoka: Innovators for the Public. Advocates argue that these terms describe the sector in its own terms, without relying on terminology used for the government or business sectors. However, use of terminology by a nonprofit of self-descriptive language that is not legally compliant risks confusing the public about nonprofit abilities, capabilities and limitations.

In some Spanish-language jurisdictions, nonprofit organizations are called 'civil associations'.

HOW TO GET STARTED STEP BY STEP

Starting a business involves planning, making key financial decisions and completing a series of legal activities. These 12 easy steps can help you plan, prepare and manage your business.

Step 1: Write a Business Plan

Use these tools and resources to create a business plan. This written guide will help you map out how you will start and run your business successfully.

Step 2: Get Business Assistance and Training

Take advantage of free training and counseling services, from preparing a business plan and securing financing, to expanding or relocating a business from the Small Business Administration.

Step 3: Choose a Business Location

Get advice on how to select a customer-friendly location and comply with zoning laws.

Step 4: Finance Your Business

Find government backed loans, venture capital and research grants to help you get started.

Step 5: Determine the Legal Structure of Your Business Decide which form of ownership is best for you: sole proprietorship, partnership, Limited Liability Company (LLC), corporation, S corporation, nonprofit or cooperative.

Step 6: Register a Business Name ("Doing Business As")
Register your business name with your state government.

Step 7: Get a Tax Identification Number

Learn which tax identification number you'll need to obtain from the IRS and your state revenue agency.

Step 8: Register for State and Local Taxes

Register with your state to obtain a tax identification number, workers' compensation, unemployment and disability insurance.

Step 9: Obtain Business Licenses and Permits

Get a list of federal, state and local licenses and permits required for your business.

Step 10: Understand Employer Responsibilities

Learn the legal steps you need to take to hire employees.

Step 11: Get Equipment and Supplies

Get everything together that you'll need in order to actually operate. This includes items such as a truck, chemicals, equipment, and the various business forms such as service contracts. Once you have these things together, you can start the marketing process in order to get new customers.

Step 12: Your Marketing Plan

Coming up with your overall marketing plan, and implementing that plan. When you're just starting, it is usually best to choose one or two major marketing strategies, and work on those until you're getting a steady stream of customers. Once you've gotten good at once specific marketing avenue, then it's a good idea to move on to another one, and repeat the process. You can begin with "Zero cost marketing" and scale up once you are bringing in constant sales.

How to Write a Business Plan

Millions of people want to know what is the secret to making money. Most have come to the conclusion that it is to start a business. So how to start a business? The first thing you do to start is business is to create a business plan.

A business plan is a formal statement of a set of business goals, the reasons they are believed attainable, and the plan for reaching those goals. It may also contain background information about the organization or team attempting to reach those goals.

A professional business plan consists of ten parts.

1. Executive Summary

The executive summary is often considered the most important section of a business plan. This section briefly tells your reader where your company is, where you want to take it, and why your business idea will be successful. If you are seeking financing, the executive summary is also your first opportunity to grab a potential investor's interest.

2. Company Description

This section of your plan provides a high-level review of the different elements of your business. This is akin to an extended elevator pitch and can help readers and potential investors quickly understand the goal of your business and its unique proposition.

3. Market Analysis

The market analysis section of your plan should illustrate your industry and market knowledge as well as any of your research findings and conclusions. This section is usually presented after the company description.

4. Organization and Management

Organization and Management follows the Market Analysis. This section should include: your company's organizational structure, details about the ownership of your company, profiles of your management team, and the qualifications of your board of directors.

5. Service or Product Line

Once you've completed the Organizational and Management section of your plan, the next part of your plan is where you describe your service or product, emphasizing the benefits to potential and current customers. Focus on why your particular product will fill a need for your target customers.

6. Marketing and Sales

Once you've completed the Service or Product Line section of your plan, the next part of your plan should focus on your marketing and sales management strategy for your business.

7. Funding Request

If you are seeking funding for your business venture, use this section to outline your requirements.

8. Financial Projections

You should develop the Financial Projections section after you've analyzed the market and set clear objectives. That's when you can allocate resources efficiently. The following is a list of the critical financial statements to include in your business plan packet.

9. Marketing and Sales

Once you've completed the Service or Product Line section of your plan, the next part of your business plan should focus on your marketing and sales management strategy for your business.

10. Appendix

The Appendix should be provided to readers on an as-needed basis. In other words, it should not be included with the main body of your business plan. Your plan is your communication tool; as such, it will be seen by a lot of people. Some of the information in the business section you will not want everyone to see, but specific individuals (such as creditors) may want access to this information to make lending decisions. Therefore, it is important to have the appendix within easy reach.

How to make your business plan stand out.

One of the first steps to business planning is determining your target market and why they would want to buy from you.

For example, is the market you serve the best one for your product or service? Are the benefits of dealing with your business clear and are they aligned with customer needs? If you're unsure about the answers to any of these questions, take a step back and revisit the foundation of your business plan.

YOUR GOLDMINE OF GOVERNMENT GRANTS!

Government grants. Many people either don't believe government grants exsist or they don't think they would ever be able to get government grant money.

First lets make one thing clear. Government grant money is **YOUR MONEY**. Government money comes from taxes paid by residents of this country. Depending on what state you live in, you are paying taxes on almost everything....Property tax for your house. Property tax on your car. Taxes on the things you purchase in the mall, or at the gas station. Taxes on your gasoline, the food you buy etc.

So get yourself in the frame of mind that you are not a charity case or too proud to ask for help, because billionaire companies like GM, Big Banks and most of Corporate America is not hesitating to get their share of **YOUR MONEY**!

There are over two thousand three hundred (2,300) Federal Government Assistance Programs. Some are loans but many are formula grants and project grants. To see all of the programs available go to:

http://www.CFDA.gov

WRITING A GRANT PROPOSAL

The Basic Components of a Proposal

There are eight basic components to creating a solid proposal package:

(5) The proposal summary;

(6)   Introduction of organization;

(7)   The problem statement

(or needs assessment);

(8)   Project objectives;

(9)   Project methods or design;

(10)   Project evaluation;

(11)   Future funding; and

(12)   The project budget.

The following will provide an overview of these components.

1. The Proposal Summary: Outline of Project Goals

The proposal summary outlines the proposed project and should appear at the beginning of the proposal. It could be in the form of a cover letter or a separate page, but should definitely be brief -- no longer than two or three paragraphs. The summary would be most useful if it were prepared after the proposal has been developed in order to encompass all the key summary points necessary to communicate the objectives of the project. It is this document that becomes the cornerstone of your proposal, and the initial impression it gives will be critical to the success of your venture. In many cases, the summary will be the first part of the proposal package seen by agency officials and very possibly could be the only part of the package that is carefully reviewed before the decision is made to consider the project any further.

The applicant must select a fundable project which can be supported in view of the local need. Alternatives, in the absence of Federal support, should be pointed out. The influence of the project both during and after the project period should be explained. The consequences of the project as a result of funding should be highlighted.

2. Introduction: Presenting a Credible Applicant or Organization

The applicant should gather data about its organization from all available sources. Most proposals require a description of an applicant's organization to describe its past and present operations. Some features to consider are:

A brief biography of board members and key staff members.

The organization's goals, philosophy, track record with other grantors, and any success stories.

The data should be relevant to the goals of the Federal grantor agency and should establish the applicant's credibility.

3. The Problem Statement: Stating the Purpose at Hand

The problem statement (or needs assessment) is a key element of a proposal that makes a clear, concise, and well-supported statement of the problem to be addressed. The best way to collect information about the problem is to conduct and document both a formal and informal needs assessment for a program in the FF-4 11-08 target or service area. The information provided should be both factual and directly related to the problem addressed by the proposal. Areas to document are:

The purpose for developing the proposal.

The beneficiaries -- who are they and how will they benefit.

The social and economic costs to be affected.

The nature of the problem (provide as much hard evidence as possible).

How the applicant organization came to realize the problem exists, and what is currently being done about the problem.

The remaining alternatives available when funding has been exhausted. Explain what will happen to the project and the impending implications.

Most importantly, the specific manner through which problems might be solved. Review the resources needed, considering how they will be used and to what end.

There is a considerable body of literature on the exact assessment techniques to be used. Any local, regional, or State government planning office, or local university offering course work in planning and evaluation techniques should be able to provide excellent background references.

Types of data that may be collected include: historical, geographic, quantitative, factual, statistical, and philosophical information, as well as studies completed by colleges, and literature searches from public or university libraries.

Local colleges or universities which have a department or section related to the proposal topic may help determine if there is interest in developing a student or faculty project to conduct a needs assessment. It may be helpful to include examples of the findings for highlighting in the proposal.

4. Project Objectives: Goals and Desired Outcome

Program objectives refer to specific activities in a proposal. It is necessary to identify all objectives related to the goals to be reached, and the methods to be employed to achieve the stated objectives. Consider quantities or things measurable and refer to a problem statement and the outcome of proposed activities when developing a well-stated objective. The figures used should be verifiable. Remember, if the proposal is funded, the stated objectives will probably be used to evaluate program progress, so be realistic. There is literature available to help identify and write program objectives.

5. Program Methods and Program Design: A Plan of Action

The program design refers to how the project is expected to work and solve the stated problem. Sketch out the following:

The activities to occur along with the related resources and staff needed to operate the project(inputs).

A flow chart of the organizational features of the project. Describe how the parts interrelate, where personnel will be needed, and what they are expected to do. Identify the kinds of facilities, transportation, and support services required (throughputs).

Explain what will be achieved through 1 and 2 above (outputs); i.e., plan for measurable results. Project staff may be required to produce evidence of program performance through an examination of stated objectives during either a site visit by the Federal grantor agency and or grant reviews which may involve peer review committees.

It may be useful to devise a diagram of the program design. For example, draw a three column block. Each column is headed by one of the parts (inputs, throughputs and outputs), and on the left 11-08 FF-5 (next to the first column) specific program features should be identified (i.e., implementation, staffing, procurement, and systems development).

In the grid, specify something about the program design, for example, assume the first column is labeled inputs and the first row is labeled staff. On the grid one might specify under inputs five nurses to operate a child care unit. The throughput might be to maintain charts, counsel the children, and set up a daily routine; outputs might be to discharge 25 healthy children per week. This type of procedure will help to conceptualize both the scope and detail of the project.

Wherever possible, justify in the narrative the course of action taken. The most economical method should be used that does not compromise or sacrifice project quality. The financial expenses associated with performance of the project will later become points of negotiation with the Federal program staff. If everything is not carefully justified in writing in the proposal, after negotiation with the Federal grantor agencies, the approved project may resemble less of the original concept.

Carefully consider the pressures of the proposed implementation, that is, the time and money needed to acquire each part of the plan. A Program Evaluation and Review Technique (PERT) chart could be useful and supportive in justifying some proposals.

The remaining alternatives available when funding has been exhausted. Explain what will happen to the project and the impending implications.

Highlight the innovative features of the proposal which could be considered distinct from other proposals under consideration.

Whenever possible, use appendices to provide details, supplementary data, references, and information requiring in-depth analysis. These types of data, although supportive of the proposal, if included in the body of the design, could detract from its readability. Appendices provide the proposal reader with immediate access to details if and when clarification of an idea, sequence or conclusion is required. Time tables, work plans, schedules, activities, methodologies, legal papers, personal vitae, letters of support, and endorsements are examples of appendices.

6. Evaluation: Product and Process Analysis

The evaluation component is two-fold: (1) product evaluation; and (2) process evaluation. Product evaluation addresses results that can be attributed to the project, as well as the extent to which the project has satisfied its desired objectives. Process evaluation addresses how the project was conducted, in terms of consistency with the stated plan of action and the effectiveness of the various activities within the plan.

Most Federal agencies now require some form of program evaluation among grantees. The requirements of the proposed project should be explored carefully. Evaluations may be conducted by an internal staff member, an evaluation firm or both. The applicant should state the amount of time needed to evaluate, how the feedback will be distributed among the proposed staff, and a schedule for review and comment for this type of communication.

Evaluation designs may start at the beginning, middle or end of a project, but the applicant should specify a start-up time. It is practical to submit an evaluation design at the start of a project for two reasons:

Convincing evaluations require the collection of appropriate data before and during program operations;

If the evaluation design cannot be prepared at the outset then a critical review of the program design may be advisable.

Even if the evaluation design has to be revised as the project progresses, it is much easier and cheaper to modify a good design. If the problem is not well defined and carefully analyzed for cause and effect relationships then a good evaluation design may be difficult to achieve. Sometimes a pilot study is needed to begin the identification of facts and relationships. Often a thorough literature search may be sufficient.

Evaluation requires both coordination and agreement among program decision makers (if known). Above all, the Federal grantor agency's requirements should be highlighted in the evaluation design. Also, Federal grantor agencies may require specific evaluation techniques such as designated data formats (an existing FF-6 11-08 information collection system) or they may offer financial inducements for voluntary participation in a national evaluation study.

The applicant should ask specifically about these points. Also, consult the Criteria For Selecting Proposals section of the Catalog program description to determine the exact evaluation methods to be required for the program if funded.

7. Future Funding: Long-Term Project Planning

Describe a plan for continuation beyond the grant period, and/or the availability of other resources necessary to implement the grant. Discuss maintenance and future program funding if program is for construction activity. Account for other needed expenditures if program includes purchase of equipment.

8.The Proposal Budget: Planning the Budget

Funding levels in Federal assistance programs change yearly. It is useful to review the appropriations over the past several years to try to project future funding levels (see Financial Information section of the Catalog program description).

However, it is safer to never anticipate that the income from the grant will be the sole support for the project. This consideration should be given to the overall budget requirements, and in particular, to budget line items most subject to inflationary pressures. Restraint is important in determining inflationary cost projections (avoid padding budget line items), but attempt to anticipate possible future increases.

Some vulnerable budget areas are: utilities, rental of buildings and equipment, salary increases, food, telephones, insurance, and transportation. Budget adjustments are sometimes made after the grant award, but this can be a lengthy process. Be certain that implementation, continuation and phase-down costs can be met. Consider costs associated with leases, evaluation systems, hard/soft match requirements, audits, development, implementation and maintenance of information and accounting systems, and other long-term financial commitments.

A well-prepared budget justifies all expenses and is consistent with the proposal narrative. Some areas in need of an evaluation for consistency are:

(13) the salaries in the proposal in relation to those of the applicant organization should be similar;

(14) if new staff persons are being hired, additional space and equipment should be considered, as necessary;

(15) if the budget calls for an equipment purchase, it should be the type allowed by the grantor agency;

(16) if additional space is rented, the increase in insurance should be supported;

(17) if an indirect cost rate applies to the proposal, the division between direct and indirect costs should not be in conflict, and the aggregate budget totals should refer directly to the approved formula; and

(18) if matching costs are required, the contributions to the matching fund should be taken out of the budget unless otherwise specified in the application instructions.

It is very important to become familiar with Government-wide circular requirements. The Catalog identifies in the program description section

(as information is provided from the agencies)

the particular circulars applicable to a Federal program, and summarizes coordination of Executive Order 12372, "Intergovernmental Review of Programs" requirements in Appendix I. The applicant should thoroughly review the appropriate circulars since they are essential in determining items such as cost principles and conforming with Government guidelines for Federal domestic assistance.

General Small Business Loans:

Loan Program, SBA's most common loan program, includes financial help for businesses with special requirements.

Loan Program Eligibility

SBA provides loans to businesses; so the requirements of eligibility are based on specific aspects of the business and its principals. As such, the key factors of eligibility are based on what the business does to receive its income, the character of its ownership and where the business operates.

SBA generally does not specify what businesses are eligible. Rather, the agency outlines what businesses are not eligible. However, there are some universally applicable requirements. To be eligible for assistance, businesses must:

Operate for profit

Be small, as defined by SBA

Be engaged in, or propose to do business in, the United States or its possessions

Have reasonable invested equity

Use alternative financial resources, including personal assets, before seeking financial assistance

Be able to demonstrate a need for the loan proceeds

Use the funds for a sound business purpose

Not be delinquent on any existing debt obligations to the U.S. Government.

Ineligible Businesses

A business must be engaged in an activity SBA determines as acceptable for financial assistance from a federal provider. The following list of businesses types are not eligible for assistance because of the activities they conduct:

Financial businesses primarily engaged in the business of lending, such as banks, finance companies, payday lenders, some leasing companies and factors (pawn shops, although engaged in lending, may qualify in some circumstances)

Businesses owned by developers and landlords that do not actively use or occupy the assets acquired or improved with the loan proceeds (except when the property is leased to the business at zero profit for the property's owners)

Life insurance companies

Businesses located in a foreign country (businesses in the U.S. owned by aliens may qualify)

Businesses engaged in pyramid sale distribution plans, where a participant's primary incentive is based on the sales made by an ever-increasing number of participants.

Businesses deriving more than one-third of gross annual revenue from legal gambling activities

Businesses engaged in any illegal activity

Private clubs and businesses that limit the number of memberships for reasons other than capacity

Government-owned entities

Businesses principally engaged in teaching, instructing, counseling or indoctrinating religion or religious beliefs, whether in a religious or secular setting

Consumer and marketing cooperatives (producer cooperatives are eligible)

Loan packagers earning more than one third of their gross annual revenue from packaging SBA loans

Businesses in which the lender or CDC, or any of its associates owns an equity interest.

Businesses that present live performances of an indecent sexual nature or derive directly or indirectly more 2.5 percent of gross revenue through the sale of products or services, or the presentation of any depictions or displays, of an indecent sexual nature

Businesses primarily engaged in political or lobbying activities

Speculative businesses (such as oil exploration)

There are also eligibility factors for financial assistance based on the activities of the owners and the historical operation of the business. As such, the business cannot have been:

A business that caused the government to have incurred a loss related to a prior business debt

A business owned 20 percent or more by a person associated with a different business that caused the government to have incurred a loss related to a prior business debt

A business owned 20 percent or more by a person who is incarcerated, on probation, on parole, or has been indicted for a felony or a crime of moral depravity.

Special Considerations

Special considerations apply to some types of businesses and individuals, which include:

Franchises are eligible except when a franchiser retains power to control operations to such an extent as to equate to an employment contract; the franchisee must have the right to profit from efforts commensurate with ownership

Recreational facilities and clubs are eligible if the facilities are open to the general public, or in membership-only situations, membership is not selectively denied or restricted to any particular groups

Farms and agricultural businesses are eligible, but these applicants should first explore Farm Service Agency (FSA) programs, particularly if the applicant has a prior or existing relationship with FSA

Fishing vessels are eligible, but those seeking funds for the construction or reconditioning of vessels with a cargo capacity of five tons or more must first request financing from the National Marine Fisheries Service

Privately owned medical facilities including hospitals, clinics, emergency outpatient facilities, and medical and dental laboratories are eligible; recovery and nursing homes are also eligible, provided they are licensed by the appropriate government agency and they provide more than room and board.

An Eligible Passive Company (EPC) must use loan proceeds to acquire or lease, and/or improve or renovate, real or personal property that it leases to one or more operating companies and must not make any profit from conducting its activities.

Legal aliens are eligible; however, consideration is given to status (e.g., resident, lawful temporary resident) in determining the business' degree of risk

Probation or parole: Applications will not be accepted from firms in which a principal is currently incarcerated, on parole, on probation or is a defendant in a criminal proceeding

Loan Amounts, Fees & Interest Rates

The specific terms of SBA loans are negotiated between a borrower and an SBA-approved lender. In general, the following provisions apply to all SBA 7(a) loans.

Loan Amounts

7(a) loans have a maximum loan amount of $5 million. SBA does not set a minimum loan amount. The average 7(a) loan amount in fiscal year 2015 was $371,628.

Fees

Loans guaranteed by the SBA are assessed a guarantee fee. This fee is based on the loan's maturity and the dollar amount guaranteed, not the total loan amount.

The lender initially pays the guaranty fee and they have the option to pass that expense on to the borrower at closing. The funds to reimburse the lender can be included in the overall loan proceeds.

On loans under $150,000 made after October 1, 2013, the fees will be set at zero percent. On any loan greater than $150,000 with a maturity of one year or shorter, the fee is 0.25 percent of the guaranteed portion of the loan.

On loans with maturities of more than one year, the normal fee is 3 percent of the SBA-guaranteed portion on loans of $150,000 to $700,000, and 3.5 percent on loans of more than $700,000. There is also an additional fee of 0.25 percent on any guaranteed portion of more than $1 million.

Interest Rates

The actual interest rate for a 7(a) loan guaranteed by the SBA is negotiated between the applicant and lender and subject to the SBA maximums. Both fixed and variable interest rate structures are available.

The maximum rate is composed of two parts, a base rate and an allowable spread. There are three acceptable base rates (A prime rate published in a daily national newspaper*, London Interbank One Month Prime plus 3 percent and an SBA Peg Rate).

Lenders are allowed to add an additional spread to the base rate to arrive at the final rate. For loans with maturities of shorter than seven years, the maximum spread will be no more than 2.25 percent.

For loans with maturities of seven years or more, the maximum spread will be 2.75 percent. The spread on loans of less than $50,000 and loans processed through Express procedures have higher maximums.

All references to the prime rate refer to the base rate in effect on the first business day of the month the loan application is received by the SBA.

Percentage of Guarantee

SBA can guarantee as much as 85 percent on loans of up to $150,000 and 75 percent on loans of more than $150,000. SBA's maximum exposure amount is $3,750,000. Thus, if a business receives an SBA-guaranteed loan for $5 million, the maximum guarantee to the lender will be $3,750,000 or 75%. SBA Express loans have a maximum guarantee set at 50 percent. 7(a) Loan Application Checklist

The specific terms of SBA loans are negotiated between a borrower and an SBA-approved lender. In general, the following provisions apply to all SBA 7(a) loans.

Loan Processing Time

There are two 7(a) loan process options with different time frames. In addition to standard procedures, SBA Express processing offers an expedited turnaround.

Special Types of 7(a) Loans

SBA offers several special purpose 7(a) loans to aid businesses that have been impacted by NAFTA, provide financial assistance to Employee Stock Ownership Plans, and help implement pollution controls.

SBA Microloan Program

The Microloan program provides loans up to $50,000 to help small businesses and certain not-for-profit childcare centers start up and expand. The average microloan is about $13,000.

The U.S. Small Business Administration provides funds to specially designated intermediary lenders, which are nonprofit community-based organizations with experience in lending as well as management and technical assistance. These intermediaries administer the Microloan program for eligible borrowers.

Eligibility Requirements

Each intermediary lender has its own lending and credit requirements. Generally, intermediaries require some type of collateral as well as the personal guarantee of the business owner.

Use of Microloan Proceeds

Microloans can be used for:

Working capital,   Inventory or supplies

Furniture or fixtures,   Machinery or equipment

Proceeds from an SBA microloan cannot be used to pay existing debts or to purchase real estate.

Repayment Terms, Interest Rates, and Fees

Loan repayment terms vary according to several factors:

Loan amount

Planned use of funds

Requirements determined by the intermediary lender

Needs of the small business borrower

The maximum repayment term allowed for an SBA microloan is six years.

Interest rates vary, depending on the intermediary lender and costs to the intermediary from the U.S. Treasury. Generally, these rates will be between 8 and 13 percent.

Application Process

Microloans are available through certain nonprofit, community-based organizations that are experienced in lending and business management assistance. If you apply for SBA microloan financing, you may be required to fulfill training or planning requirements before your loan application is considered. This business training is designed to help you launch or expand your business.

Find a Microloan Provider

To apply for a Microloan, you must work with an SBA approved intermediary in your area. Approved intermediaries make all credit decisions on SBA microloans. For more information, you can contact your local SBA District Office.

Business Legal Structure

When you are starting a business, one of the first decisions you have to make is the type of business you want to create. A sole proprietorship? A corporation? A limited liability company? This decision is important, because the type of business you create determines the types of applications you’ll need to submit. You should also research liability implications for personal investments you make into your business, as well as the taxes you will need to pay. It’s important to understand each business type and select the one that is best suited for your situation and objectives. Keep in mind that you may need to contact several federal agencies, as well as your state business entity registration office.

Here is a list of the most common ways to structure a business.

An S corporation (sometimes referred to as an S Corp) is a special type of corporation created through an IRS tax election. An eligible domestic corporation can avoid double taxation (once to the corporation and again to the shareholders) by electing to be treated as an S corporation.

A partnership is a single business where two or more people share ownership.

Each partner contributes to all aspects of the business, including money, property, labor or skill. In return, each partner shares in the profits and losses of the business.

A limited liability company is a hybrid type of legal structure that provides the limited liability features of a corporation and the tax efficiencies and operational flexibility of a partnership.

The "owners" of an LLC are referred to as "members." Depending on the state, the members can consist of a single individual (one owner), two or more individuals, corporations or other LLCs.

Corporation (C Corporation)

A corporation (sometimes referred to as a C corporation) is an independent legal entity owned by shareholders. This means that the corporation itself, not the shareholders that own it, is held legally liable for the actions and debts the business incurs.

Corporations are more complex than other business structures because they tend to have costly administrative fees and complex tax and legal requirements. Because of these issues, corporations are generally suggested for established, larger companies with multiple employees.

A cooperative is a business or organization owned by and operated for the benefit of those using its services. Profits and earnings generated by the cooperative are distributed among the members, also known as user-owners.

Typically, an elected board of directors and officers run the cooperative while regular members have voting power to control the direction of the cooperative. Members can become part of the cooperative by purchasing shares, though the amount of shares they hold does not affect the weight of their vote.

Selecting The Right Business Name

Ask 500 people already in business how they decided upon their business name and you will get 500 different answers. Everyone has a story behind how they chose their own business name. Even if the business is named after their own birth name, there's a reason why this was done.

When you open a business, in a sense, you are causing a new birth to begin. This new birth was created from an idea alone by you or your associates. It will have its own bank account, it's own federal identification number, it's own credit accounts, it's own income and it's own bills. On paper, it is another individual! Just as if you were choosing a name for your own unborn child, you need to spend considerable time in deciding upon your business name.

There are several reasons why a good business name is vitally important to your business. The first obvious reason is because it is the initial identification to your customers. No one would want to do business with someone if they didn't have a company name yet.

This makes you look like an amateur who is very unreliable. Even if you call your company "Kevin's Lawn Service," a company name has been established and you are indeed a company. People will therefore feel more comfortable dealing with you.

Secondly, a business name normally is an indication as to the product or service you offer. "Mary's Typing Service," "Karate Club for Men," "Jim-Dandy Jack-of-all-Trades," "Laurie and Steve's Laundry," "Misty's Gift Boutique," and "Star 1 Publishers" are all examples of simple business names that immediately tell the customer what product you offer.

However, most people will choose the simple approach when naming their business. They use their name, their spouse's name, their children's names or a combination of these names when naming a business. The national hamburger-restaurant chain "Wendy's" was named after the owner's daughter.

However, research has proven that these "cutesy" names are not the best names to use for a business. Many experts claim that it makes the business look too "mom-and-pop-sie." However, this depends on the business. If you are selling something that demands this mood or theme to appeal to your market, it's best to use this approach.

Personally, I am inclined to name my businesses with catchy names that stick in people's heads after we have initially made contact. Names like, "Sensible Solutions," "Direct Defenders," "Moonlighters Ink," "Printer's Friend," "Strictly Class," "Collections and Treasures," and "Starlight on Twilight" are all good examples of catchy names. These types of names relate to your product or service but serve as a type of slogan for your business. This is a big help when marketing.

A friend I know owns a business called "Mint and Pepper." He grows and sells his own line of raw seasonings to people in the local area. At a get-together for small businesses, he passed out his business card. The card had a peppermint candy glued on the back and the slogan read: "Your business is worth a mint to us." This marketing concept not only got my friend noticed and remembered, but brought in several large orders for the business.

When you name a child, you may not decide upon a definite name until after they are born. You do this because a name is sometimes associated with a type of personality. When you name a business you may need to wait until you have a product or service to sell and then decide upon a business name before going into the business itself because your business name should give some clue as to what product or service you are selling.

A business named "Joe's Collections" normally wouldn't sell car parts and a business named "Charlie Horse" would not sell knitting supplies.

To generate ideas - begin looking at business signs everywhere you go. Notice which ones catch your eye and stick in your mind. Try and figure out "why" they stuck in your mind. Naturally, the business "Dominos Pizza" sticks in your mind because it is nationally known. These don't count!

Look around and notice the smaller businesses. Take your time. Within a few days you should be able to come up with a few potential business names.

Then, when you finally find a few names you really like - try reciting them to other people and get their opinion. It won't be long until your business will have the proper name that will carry it through it's life!

HINT:

Try to avoid very long names so they will fit into small display ads. Amalgamated International Enterprises can be easily presented as AIE - which is easier and shorter to spell.

Register Your Business Name

Naming your business is an important branding exercise, but if you choose to name your business as anything other than your own personal name then you'll need to register it with the appropriate authorities.

This process is known as registering your "Doing Business As" (DBA) name.

What is a "Doing Business As" Name?

A fictitious name (or assumed name, trade name or DBA name) is a business name that is different from your personal name, the names of your partners or the officially registered name of your LLC or corporation.

It's important to note that when you form a business, the legal name of the business defaults to the name of the person or entity that owns the business, unless you choose to rename it and register it as a DBA name.

For example, consider this scenario: John Smith sets up a painting business. Rather than operate under his own name, John instead chooses to name his business: "John Smith Painting". This name is considered an assumed name and John will need to register it with the appropriate local government agency. The legal name of your business is required on all government forms and applications, including your application for employer tax IDs, licenses and permits.

Do I Need a "Doing Business As" Name?

A DBA is needed in the following scenarios:

Sole Proprietors or Partnerships – If you wish to start a business under anything other than your real name, you'll need to register a DBA so that you can do business as another name.

Existing Corporations or LLCs – If your business is already set up and you want to do business under a name other than your existing corporation or LLC name, you will need to register a DBA.

Note: Not all states require the registering of fictitious business names or DBAs.

Registering your DBA is done either with your county clerk's office or with your state government, depending on where your business is located. There are a few states that do not require the registering of fictitious business names.

Business Tax Advantages

Every year, several thousand people develop an interest in "going into business." Many of these people have an idea, a product or a service they hope to promote into an income producing business
which they can operate from their homes.

If you are one of these people, here are some practical thoughts to consider before hanging out the "Open for Business" sign.

In areas zoned "Residential Only," your proposed business could be illegal. In many areas, zoning restrictions rule out home businesses involving the coming and going of many customers,clients or employees. Many businesses that sell or even store
anything for sale on the premises also fall into this category.

Be sure to check with your local zoning office to see how the ordinances in your particular area may affect your business plans. You may need a special permit to operate your business from your home; and you may find that making small changes in your plan will put you into the position of meeting zoning
standards.

Many communities grant home occupation permits for businesses involve typing, sewing, and teaching, but turn thumbs down on requests from photographers, interior decorators and home improvement businesses to be run from the home.

And often, even if you are permitted to use your home for a given business, there will be restrictions that you may need to take into consideration. By all means, work with your zoning people, and save yourself time, trouble and dollars.

One of the requirements imposed might be off street parking for your customers or patrons. And, signs are generally forbidden in residential districts. If you teach, there is almost always a limit on the number of students you may have at any one time.

Obtaining zoning approval for your business, then, could be as simple as filling out an application, or it could involve a public hearing. The important points the zoning officials will consider will center around how your business will affect the neighborhood. Will it increase the traffic noticeably on your street? Will there be a substantial increase in noise? And how will your neighbors feel about this business alongside their homes?

To repeat, check into the zoning restrictions, and then check again to determine if you will need a city license. If you're selling something, you may need a vendor's license, and be required to collect sales taxes on your transactions. The sale tax requirement would result in the need for careful record keeping.

Licensing can be an involved process, and depending upon the type of business, it could even involve the inspection of your home to determine if it meets with local health and building and fire codes. Should this be the case, you will need to bring your facilities up to the local standards. Usually this will involve some simple repairs or adjustments that you can either do personally, or hire out to a handyman at a nominal cost.

Still more items to consider: Will your homeowner's insurance cover the property and liability in your new business? This must definitely be resolved, so be sure to talk it over with your insurance agent.

Tax deductions, which were once one of the beauties of engaging in a home business, are not what they once were. To be eligible for business related deductions today, you must use that part of your home claimed EXCLUSIVELY AND REGULARLY as either the principal location of your business, or place reserved to meet patients, clients or customers.

An interesting case in point: if you use your den or a spare bedroom as the principal place of business, working there from 8:00 to 5:00 every day, but permit your children to watch TV in that room during evening hours, the IRS dictates that you cannot claim a deduction for that room as your office or place of business.

There are, however, a couple of exceptions to the "exclusive use" rule. One is the storage on inventory in your home, where your home is the location of your trade or business, and your trade or business is the selling of products at retail or wholesale.

According to the IRS, such storage space must be used on a REGULAR Basis, and be separately identifiable space.

Another exception applies to daycare services that are provided for children, the elderly, or physically or mentally handicapped. This exception applies only if the owner of the facility complies with the state laws for licensing.

To be eligible for business deductions, your business must be an activity undertaken with the intent of making profit. It's presumed you meet this requirement if your business makes a profit in any two years of a five-year period.

Once you are this far along, you can deduct business expenses such as supplies, subscriptions to professional journals, and an allowance for the business use of your car or truck. You can also
claim deductions for home related business expenses such as utilities, and in some cases, even a new paint job for your home.

The IRS is going to treat the part of your home you use for business as though it were a separate piece of property. This means that you'll have to keep good records and take care not to mix business and personal matters. No specific method of record
keeping is required, but your records must clearly justify and deductions you claim.

You can begin by calculating what percentage of the house is used for business, Either by number of rooms or by area in square footage. Thus, if you use one of the five rooms for your business, the business portion is 20 percent. If you run your business out of a room that's 10 by 12 feet, and the total area of your home is 1,200 square feet, the business space factor is 10 percent.

An extra computation is required if your business is a home day care center. This is one of the exempted activities in which the exclusive use rule doesn't apply. Check with your tax preparer and the IRS for an exact determination.

If you're a renter, you can deduct the part of your rent which is attributable to the business share of your house or apartment. Homeowners can take a deduction based on the depreciation of the business portion of their house.

There is a limit to the amount you can deduct. This is the amount equal to the gross income generated by the business, minus those home expenses you could deduct even if you weren't operating a business from your home. As an example, real estate taxes and mortgage interest are deductible regardless of any business Activity in your home, so you must subtract from your business Gross income the percentage that's allocable to the business portion of your home. You thus arrive at the maximum amount for home-related business deductions.

If you are self-employed, you claim your business deductions on SCHEDULE C, PROFIT(or LOSS) for BUSINESS OR PROFESSION. The IRS emphasizes that claiming business-at-home deductions does not automatically trigger an audit on your tax return.

Even so, it is always wise to keep meticulously within the proper guidelines, and of course keep detailed records if you claim business related expenses when you are working out of your home. You should discuss this aspect of your operation with your tax preparer or a person qualified in the field of small business tax requirements.

If your business earnings aren't subject to withholding tax, and your estimated federal taxes are $100 or more, you'll probably be filing a Declaration of Estimated Tax, Form 1040 ES.

To complete this form, you will have to estimate your income for the coming year and also make a computation of the income tax and self-employed tax you will owe.

The self-employment taxes pay for Social Security coverage. If you have a salaried job covered by Social Security, the self-employment tax applies only to that amount of your home business income that, when added to your salary, reaches the current ceiling. When you file your Form 1040-ES, which is due April 15, you must make the first of four equal installment payments on your estimated tax bill.

Another good way to trim taxes is by setting up a Keogh plan or an Individual Retirement Account. With either of these, you can shelter some of your home business income from taxes by investing it for your retirement.

HOW TO HIRE YOUR EMPLOYEE'S

If your business is booming, but you are struggling to keep up, perhaps it's time to hire some help.

The eight steps below can help you start the hiring process and ensure you are compliant with key federal and state regulations.

Step 1. Obtain an Employer Identification Number (EIN)

Before hiring your first employee, you need to get an employment identification number (EIN) from the U.S. Internal Revenue Service. The EIN is often referred to as an Employer Tax ID or as Form SS-4. The EIN is necessary for reporting taxes and other documents to the IRS. In addition, the EIN is necessary when reporting information about your employees to state agencies. Apply for EIN online or contact the IRS at 1-800-829-4933.

Step 2. Set up Records for Withholding Taxes

According to the IRS, you must keep records of employment taxes for at least four years. Keeping good records can also help you monitor the progress of your business, prepare financial statements, identify sources of receipts, keep track of deductible expenses, prepare your tax returns, and support items reported on tax returns.

Below are three types of withholding taxes you need for your business:

Federal Income Tax Withholding

Every employee must provide an employer with a signed withholding exemption certificate (Form W-4) on or before the date of employment. The employer must then submit Form W-4 to the IRS. For specific information, read the IRS' Employer's Tax Guide.

Federal Wage and Tax Statement

Every year, employers must report to the federal government wages paid and taxes withheld for each employee. This report is filed using Form W-2, wage and tax statement. Employers must complete a W-2 form for each employee who they pay a salary, wage or other compensation.

Employers must send Copy A of W-2 forms to the Social Security Administration by the last day of February to report wages and taxes of your employees for the previous calendar year. In addition, employers should send copies of W-2 forms to their employees by Jan. 31 of the year following the reporting period. Visit SSA.gov/employer for more information.

State Taxes

Depending on the state where your employees are located, you may be required to withhold state income taxes. Visit the state and local tax page for more information.

Step 3. Employee Eligibility Verification

Federal law requires employers to verify an employee's eligibility to work in the United States. Within three days of hire, employers must complete Form I-9, employment eligibility verification, which requires employers to examine documents to confirm the employee's citizenship or eligibility to work in the U.S. Employers can only request documentation specified on the I-9 form.

Employers do not need to submit the I-9 form with the federal government but are required to keep them on file for three years after the date of hire or one year after the date of the employee's termination, whichever is later.

Employers can use information taken from the Form I-9 to electronically verify the employment eligibility of newly hired employees by registering with E-Verify.

Visit the U.S. Immigration and Customs Enforcement agency's I-9 website to download the form and find more information.

Step 4. Register with Your State's New Hire Reporting Program

All employers are required to report newly hired and re-hired employees to a state directory within 20 days of their hire or rehire date.

Step 5. Obtain Workers' Compensation Insurance

All businesses with employees are required to carry workers' compensation insurance coverage through a commercial carrier, on a self-insured basis or through their state's Workers' Compensation Insurance program.

Step 6. Post Required Notices

Employers are required to display certain posters in the workplace that inform employees of their rights and employer responsibilities under labor laws. Visit the Workplace Posters page for specific federal and state posters you'll need for your business.

Step 7. File Your Taxes

Generally, employers who pay wages subject to income tax withholding, Social Security and Medicare taxes must file IRS Form 941, Employer's Quarterly Federal Tax Return. For more information, visit IRS.gov.

New and existing employers should consult the IRS Employer's Tax Guide to understand all their federal tax filing requirements.

Step 8. Get Organized and Keep Yourself Informed

Being a good employer doesn't stop with fulfilling your various tax and reporting obligations. Maintaining a healthy and fair workplace, providing benefits and keeping employees informed about your company's policies are key to your business' success. Here are some additional steps you should take after you've hired your first employee:

Set up Recordkeeping

In addition to requirements for keeping payroll records of your employees for tax purposes, certain federal employment laws also require you to keep records about your employees. The following sites provide more information about federal reporting requirements:

Tax Recordkeeping Guidance

Labor Recordkeeping Requirements

Occupational Safety and Health Act Compliance

Employment Law Guide (employee benefits chapter)

Apply Standards that Protect Employee Rights

Complying with standards for employee rights in regards to equal opportunity and fair labor standards is a requirement. Following statutes and regulations for minimum wage, overtime, and child labor will help you avoid error and a lawsuit. See the Department of Labor's Employment Law Guide for up-to-date information on these statutes and regulations.

Also, visit the Equal Employment Opportunity Commission and Fair Labor Standards Act.

Web Wholesale Resource Rolodex

As of the writting of this book all, of the companies below, website is up and have an active business. From time to time companies go out of business or change their web address. So, instead of just giving you just 1 source I give you plenty to choose from.

NONPROFIT RESOURCES

https://www.501commons.org/resources/overview

http://www.nonprofitcareer.com/director.htm

http://npod.org/

http://www.libraryspot.com/directories/nonprofits.htm

FUNDRAISING

https://www.fundraise.com/non-profit

https://doublethedonation.com/fundraising-ideas/

https://goo.gl/wf3z6W

http://www.abcfundraising.com/

Accounting Software

https://goo.gl/W5uNlN

http://findaccountingsoftware.com/

http://www.software4nonprofits.com/download.htm

https://goo.gl/oHZCfO

https://goo.gl/q7jyku

TRANSPORTATION

Used Trucks/CARS Online

http://gsaauctions.gov/gsaauctions/gsaauctions/

http://www.ebay.com/motors

http://www.uhaul.com/TruckSales/

http://www.usedtrucks.ryder.com/vehicle/Vehicle
Search.aspx?VehicleTypeId=1&VehicleGroupId=3

http://www.penskeusedtrucks.com/truck-
types/light-and-medium-duty/

Parts

http://www.truckchamp.com/

http://www.autopartswarehouse.com/

Bikes & Motorcycles

http://gsaauctions.gov/gsaauctions/aucindx/

http://www.bikesdirect.com/products/used-bikes/?gclid=CLCF0vaDm7kCFYtDMgodzW0AXQ

http://www.overstock.com/Sports-Toys/Cycling/450/cat.html

http://www.nashbar.com/bikes/TopCategories_10053_htt
p://www.nashbar.com/bikes/TopCategories_10053_1005
2_-110052_-1

http://www.bti-usa.com/

http://evosales.com/

COMPUTERS/Office Equipment

http://www.wtsmedia.com/

http://www.laptopplaza.com/

http://www.outletpc.com/

Computer Tool Kits

http://www.dhgate.com/wholesale/computer+repair+tools.html

http://www.aliexpress.com/wholesale/wholesale-repair-computer-tool.html

http://wholesalecomputercables.com/Computer-Repair-Tool-Kit/M/B00006OXGZ.htm

http://www.tigerdirect.com/applications/category/category_tlc.asp?CatId=47&name=Computer%20Tools

Computer Parts

http://www.laptopuniverse.com/

http://www.sabcal.com/

other

http://www.nearbyexpress.com/

http://www.commercialbargains.co

http://www.getpaid2workfromhome.com

http://www.boyerblog.com/success-tools

American merchandise liquidators

http://www.amlinc.com/

the closeout club

http://www.thecloseoutclub.com/

RJ discount sales

http://www.rjsks.com/

St louis wholesale

http://www.stlouiswholesale.com/

Wholesale Electronics

http://www.weisd.com/

http://www.anawholesale.com/

office wholesale

http://www.1-computerdesks.com/

1aaa wholesale merchandise

http://www.1aaawholesalemerchandise.com/

big lots wholesale

http://www.biglotswholesale.com/

More Business Resources

1.   http://www.sba.gov/content/starting-green-business

home based businesses

2.   http://www.sba.gov/content/home-based-business

3.   online businesses

http://www.sba.gov/content/setting-online-business

4.   self employed and independent contractors

http://www.sba.gov/content/self-employed-independent-contractors

5.   minority owned businesses

http://www.sba.gov/content/minority-owned-businesses

6.   veteran owned businesses

http://www.sba.gov/content/veteran-service-disabled-veteran-owned

7. woman owned businesses

http://www.sba.gov/content/women-owned-businesses

8. people with disabilities

http://www.sba.gov/content/people-with-disabilities

9. young entrepreneurs

http://www.sba.gov/content/young-entrepreneurs

ZERO COST MARKETING

The web-RESOURCE guide has plenty of web sites for you to find products at huge dicounts. Below are a few steps to market those products using
ZERO COST INTERNET MARKETING stratigies.

While there are many ways to market we are only going focuse on ZERO COST MARKETING. You are starting up. You can always go for the more expensive ways of marketing after your business is producing income.

FREE WEB HOSTING

Get a free web site. You can get a free web site at weebly.com or wix.com. Or just type "free web hosting" in a google, bing or yahoo search engine.

Free web hosting is something you can use for a varitey or reasons. However many free web hosting sites add an extention to the name of you web address that lets everyone know you are using their services. For this reason you eventually want to scale up once you start making income.

LOW COST PAID WEB HOSTING

Free is nice, but you when you need to expand your business it is best to go with a paid web hosting service. There are several that give you good value for under $10.00 a month.

1. Yahoo small business

2. Intuit.com

3. ipage.com

4. Hostgator.com

5. Godaddy.com

Yahoo small business allows for unlimited web pages and is probably the best overall value, but they require a years payment up front. Intuit allows for monthly payments.

For free ecommerce on your web site, open up a Paypal account and get the HTML code for payment buttons for free. Then put those buttons on your web site.

Step by Step basic zero cost web site traffic instructions

Step 1 zero cost internet marketing

Now that your web site is up and running you should register it with at least the top 3 search engines. 1. Google 2. Bing 3. Yahoo.

Step 2 zero cost internet marketing

Write and submit a press release. Google "free press release sites" for press release sites that will allow you to summit press releases for free. I you do not know how to write a press release go to www.fiverr.com and sub-contract the work out for only $5.00 !!!

Step 3 zero cost internet marketing

Write and submit articles to article marketing web sites like ezinearticles.com.

Step 4 zero cost internet marketing

Create and submit videos to video sharing sites like dailymotion.com or youtube.com. Make sure to include a hyperlink to your website in the description of your videos.

Step 5 zero cost internet marketing

Submit your web site to dmoz.org. This is a huge open directory that many smaller search engines go to get web sites for their database.

Getting Motivated to Start Your Business

The other day I was driving down a street in a commercial district and noticed a moving van. Two "blue collar workers" were busy loading office furniture in a company-owned vehicle. It was obvious that they were employees of this major company and I surmised they were making about $12 per hour.

I then thought about the normal lives these men probably lived. They had to punch a time-clock every day. If they were sick, they had to report to a boss and get permission to stay home. They had to depend on the company to pay them a weekly salary. They got paid the same amount of money every week and were lucky to get a raise every year or so.

Because of being controlled by a time clock at work, they naturally arranged their lives in the same fashion. They came home at the same time, ate dinner at the same time, looked forward to Friday for 2 days of rest but ended up cramming all their neglected responsibilities from the previous week into those 2 days.

The entire human race consists of two major groups of people: (1) Leaders and (2) Followers. Leaders have a built-in knack to not be happy with the normal flow of existence. Leaders are continually striving for a way out of this rat-race because they have a human characteristic of wanting to lead instead of follow.

But a good many of these leaders don't have a lot of money because they have been working for an employer all their lives. They recognize that they will never achieve the level of success they desire working for someone else. But they can't just leave their job and survive on their own. How could they pay the rent? Put their children through college? Buy the groceries? Pay Visa and Mastercard? With all these fears sitting in the leader will often exist as a follower because he or she doesn't believe they have a choice.

But they do! In fact, the answer is right under their noses. Allow me to explain . . .

Let's take the guy working for the moving company that I saw when I was driving down the street. He could offer the same service on weekends through word-of-mouth advertising. By placing a simple classified ad under Services Offered in the local newspaper, he could pick up a couple jobs a month and bring in an extra income.

Or how about the lady that just had a baby and wants to stay at home with it. Her maternity leave from her employer, only allows her 6 weeks. If she doesn't go back to work then she will either lose her job, her income or both. If her husband doesn't bring in enough money to support her and the baby she doesn't think she has a choice. The new mother will sacrifice money for her child.

But if this lady wants to stay at home with her child, why doesn't she start a home day-care center? That way, she would still make money and be able to be with her new child at the same time. Good for the child. Good for the mother.

Good for the family unit. Good for other working mothers who can trust a "mother-run" day care center versus a commercial one. Plus since the day care center is in this mother's home, she can charge 40% to 50% less than commercial day care centers and probably make more money compared to her old job.

Too often, people who want to break out of the mold and start their own business will seek for products and services they know absolutely nothing about. Someone told them they could make a lot of money doing this and doing that. But the truth is that it will take anyone longer to make money with a product or service that they have to learn. In fact, this learning period could take a year or more.

The person could easily be discouraged about a small business if it doesn't make any money by then.

So, if you are considering starting a small business; entertain the possibility of starting one based on the skills you already possess.

BONUS MATERIAL: CREDIT REPAIR

Credit can sometimes be the lifeblood of a business, but today many simply don't know their rights when it comes to credit.

The information below from the FTC (Federal Trade Commission) can help you to get a FREE CREDIT REPORT and begin to correct or remove any blemishes on your credit.

The Fair Credit Reporting Act (FCRA) requires each of the nationwide credit reporting companies — Equifax, Experian, and TransUnion — to provide you with a free copy of your credit report, at your request, once every 12 months. The FCRA promotes the accuracy and privacy of information in the files of the nation's credit reporting companies. The Federal Trade Commission (FTC), the nation's consumer protection agency, enforces the FCRA with respect to credit reporting companies.

A credit report includes information on where you live, how you pay your bills, and whether you've been sued or have filed for bankruptcy. Nationwide credit reporting companies sell the information in your report to creditors, insurers, employers, and other businesses that use it to evaluate your applications for credit, insurance, employment, or renting a home.

Here are the details about your rights under the FCRA, which established the free annual credit report program.

Q: How do I order my free report?

The three nationwide credit reporting companies have set up a central website, a toll-free telephone number, and a mailing address through which you can order your free annual report.

To order, visit annualcreditreport.com, call 1-877-322-8228. Or complete the Annual Credit Report https://www.consumer.ftc.gov/articles/pdf-0093-annual-report-request-form.pdfRequest Form and mail it to: Annual Credit Report Request Service, P.O. Box 105281, Atlanta, GA 30348-5281. Do not contact the three nationwide credit reporting companies individually. They are providing free annual credit reports only through annualcreditreport.com, 1-877-322-8228 or mailing to Annual Credit Report Request Service.

You may order your reports from each of the three nationwide credit reporting companies at the same time, or you can order your report from each of the companies one at a time. The law allows you to order one free copy of your report from each of the nationwide credit reporting companies every 12 months.

A Warning About "Imposter" Websites

Only one website is authorized to fill orders for the free annual credit report you are entitled to under law — annualcreditreport.com. Other websites that claim to offer "free credit reports," "free credit scores," or "free credit monitoring" are not part of the legally mandated free annual credit report program.

In some cases, the "free" product comes with strings attached. For example, some sites sign you up for a supposedly "free" service that converts to one you have to pay for after a trial period. If you don't cancel during the trial period, you may be unwittingly agreeing to let the company start charging fees to your credit card.

Some "imposter" sites use terms like "free report" in their names; others have URLs that purposely misspell annualcreditreport.com in the hope that you will mistype the name of the official site. Some of these "imposter" sites direct you to other sites that try to sell you something or collect your personal information.

Annualcreditreport.com and the nationwide credit reporting companies will not send you an email asking for your personal information. If you get an email, see a pop-up ad, or get a phone call from someone claiming to be from annualcreditreport.com or any of the three nationwide credit reporting companies, do not reply or click on any link in the message. It's probably a scam. Forward any such email to the FTC at   spam@uce.gov.

Q: What information do I need to provide to get my free report?

A: You need to provide your name, address, Social Security number, and date of birth. If you have moved in the last two years, you may have to provide your previous address. To maintain the security of your file, each nationwide credit reporting company may ask you for some information that only you would know, like the amount of your monthly mortgage payment.

Each company may ask you for different information because the information each has in your file may come from different sources.

Q: Why do I want a copy of my credit report?

A: Your credit report has information that affects whether you can get a loan — and how much you will have to pay to borrow money. You want a copy of your credit report to:

☐ make sure the information is accurate, complete, and up-to-date before you apply for a loan for a major purchase like a house or car, buy insurance, or apply for a job.

☐ help guard against identity theft. That's when someone uses your personal information — like your name, your Social Security number, or your credit card number — to commit fraud. Identity thieves may use your information to open a new credit card account in your name. Then, when they don't pay the bills, the delinquent account is reported on your credit report. Inaccurate information like that could affect your ability to get credit, insurance, or even a job.

Q: How long does it take to get my report after I order it?

A: If you request your report online at annualcreditreport.com, you should be able to access it immediately. If you order your report by calling toll-free 1-877-322-8228, your report will be processed and mailed to you within 15 days. If you order your report by mail using the Annual Credit Report Request Form, your request will be processed and mailed to you within 15 days of receipt.

Whether you order your report online, by phone, or by mail, it may take longer to receive your report if the nationwide credit reporting company needs more information to verify your identity.

Q: Are there any other situations where I might be eligible for a free report?

A: Under federal law, you're entitled to a free report if a company takes adverse action against you, such as denying your application for credit, insurance, or employment, and you ask for your report within 60 days of receiving notice of the action. The notice will give you the name, address, and phone number of the credit reporting company.

You're also entitled to one free report a year if you're unemployed and plan to look for a job within 60 days; if you're on welfare; or if your report is inaccurate because of fraud, including identity theft. Otherwise, a credit reporting company may charge you a reasonable amount for another copy of your report within a 12-month period.

To buy a copy of your report, contact:

☐ Equifax:1-800-685-1111; equifax.com
☐ Experian: 1-888-397-3742; experian.com
☐ TransUnion: 1-800-916-8800; transunion.com

Q: Should I order a report from each of the three nationwide credit reporting companies?

A: It's up to you. Because nationwide credit reporting companies get their information from different sources, the information in your report from one company may not reflect all, or the same, information in your reports from the other two companies. That's not to say that the information in any of your reports is necessarily inaccurate; it just may be different.

Q: Should I order my reports from all three of the nationwide credit reporting companies at the same time?

A: You may order one, two, or all three reports at the same time, or you may stagger your requests. It's your choice. Some financial advisors say staggering your requests during a 12-month period may be a good way to keep an eye on the accuracy and completeness of the information in your reports.

Q: What if I find errors — either inaccuracies or incomplete information — in my credit report?

A: Under the FCRA, both the credit report ing company and the information provider (that is, the person, company, or organization that provides information about you to a consumer reporting company) are responsible for correcting inaccurate or incomplete information in your report. To take full advantage of your rights under this law, contact the credit reporting company and the information provider.

1. Tell the credit reporting company, in writing, what information you think is inaccurate.

Credit reporting companies must investigate the items in question — usually within 30 days — unless they consider your dispute frivolous. They also must forward all the relevant data you provide about the inaccuracy to the organization that provided the information. After the information provider receives notice of a dispute from the credit reporting company, it must investigate, review the relevant information, and report the results back to the credit reporting company. If the information provider finds the disputed information is inaccurate, it must notify all three nationwide credit reporting companies so they can correct the information in your file.

When the investigation is complete, the credit reporting company must give you the written results and a free copy of your report if the dispute results in a change. (This free report does not count as your annual free report.) If an item is changed or deleted, the credit reporting company cannot put the disputed information back in your file unless the information provider verifies that it is accurate and complete. The credit reporting company also must send you written notice that includes the name, address, and phone number of the information provider.

2. Tell the creditor or other information provider in writing that you dispute an item. Many providers specify an address for disputes. If the provider reports the item to a credit reporting company, it must include a notice of your dispute. And if you are correct — that is, if the information is found to be inaccurate — the information provider may not report it again.

Q: What can I do if the credit reporting company or information provider won't correct the information I dispute?

A: If an investigation doesn't resolve your dispute with the credit reporting company, you can ask that a statement of the dispute be included in your file and in future reports. You also can ask the credit reporting company to provide your state ment to anyone who received a copy of your report in the recent past. You can expect to pay a fee for this service.

If you tell the information provider that you dispute an item, a notice of your dispute must be included any time the information provider reports the item to a credit reporting company.

Q: How long can a credit reporting company report negative information?

A: A credit reporting company can report most accurate negative information for seven years and bankruptcy information for 10 years. There is no time limit on reporting information about criminal convictions; information reported in response to your application for a job that pays more than $75,000 a year; and information reported because you've applied for more than $150,000 worth of credit or life insurance. Information about a lawsuit or an unpaid judgment against you can be reported for seven years or until the statute of limitations runs out, whichever is longer.

Q: Can anyone else get a copy of my credit report?

A: The FCRA specifies who can access your credit report. Creditors, insurers, employers, and other businesses that use the information in your report to evaluate your applications for credit, insurance, employment, or renting a home are among those that have a legal right to access your report.

Q: Can my employer get my credit report?

A: Your employer can get a copy of your credit report only if you agree. A credit reporting company may not provide information about you to your employer, or to a prospective employer, without your written consent.

For More Information

The FTC works for the consumer to prevent fraudulent, deceptive, and unfair business practices in the marketplace and to provide information to help consumers spot, stop, and avoid them. To file a complaint, visit ftc.gov/complaint or call 1-877-FTC-HELP (1-877-382-4357).

Get Our Video Training Program at:

(Zero Cost Internet Marketing complete 142 video series)

http://goo.gl/gQnSo4

Massive Money for Real Estate Investing

http://www.BrianSMahoney.com